The offices of *The Manchester Guardian*,
Cross Street, 17 December 1902.

BYGONE MANCHESTER

Bygone Manchester

Eric Krieger

Phillimore

1984

Published by
PHILLIMORE & CO. LTD.
Shopwyke Hall, Chichester, Sussex

ISBN 0 85033 537 X

Printed and bound in Great Britain by
BIDDLES LTD
Guildford and King's Lynn

ACKNOWLEDGEMENTS

Many of the illustrations in this book are taken from old postcards in the author's own collection. It would have been impossible to acquire these souvenirs of yesteryear without the diligent searching of dealers too numerous to list.

In preparing the notes and captions one was constantly thankful for the researches of others. Several excellent essays on the development of Manchester from Roman times are included in C. F. Carter (ed.), *Manchester and its Region* (1962). Michael Kennedy's *Portrait of Manchester* (1970) is an affectionate account of the city and a source of much information. The *Soul of Manchester*, edited by W. H. Brindley (1929) provides a perspective from the inter-war years. Nikolaus Pevsner's *Buildings of England* has been a valued architectural guide. The *Manchester Evening News* and *Manchester Guardian* have given a contemporary freshness to several events. Sarah Wilson made a much appreciated trek to the Colindale Newspaper Library in the hunt for information.

F. W. Woolworth & Co., both the Manchester, Piccadilly, branch and the London head-office, were kind enough to reply to my enquiries. Allan Barlow of the Manchester Central Library Local History Department deserves especial mention for his hard work and help. Fred Humphreys took the trouble and time to photocopy several articles on the tribulations of Belle Vue. I also wish to thank Rolls Royce Ltd. for their permission to use plates 111 to 120 inclusive.

My thanks are offered to all who have assisted in the compiling of this book, but they are of course, in no way responsible for any resulting errors or flaws. I would finally like to express my gratitude for the interest shown in this project by Phillimore.

LIST OF ILLUSTRATIONS

INTRODUCTION

Agricola to Victoria

The name Manchester itself betrays the city's Roman antecedents. A more pervasive, if less tangible heritage than the excavations at Castlefield, it comes down to us as the result of several mutilations of *Mamucium* 'place of the breast-like hill', such as *Mancunium*. The Roman fort was built during the time of Agricola (A.D. 78-86), on the road linking the legionary encampments at York and Chester.

Continuity of growth is not recorded until medieval times. In the 10th century, Edward the Elder is noted as having sent a force to repair and defend the old fort against Norse incursions. The Domesday survey of 1086 gives Manchester as an inferior manor of the Salford Hundred. The emerging town was sited not by the Roman fort, but around the present cathedral at the confluence of the Irwell and the Irk. Manorial rights were first conferred on the Grelley family, who built a fortified hall. In the 13th century an annual fair was granted on Acresfield (Saint Ann's Square) and the lord of the manor owned both corn and fulling mills on the Irk, suggesting the craft of wool-weaving. Although Manchester was awarded a charter in 1301, a jury of northern landowners ruled in 1359 that it was not a borough but a market town. Thomas Grelley died without a male heir and the manor passed to the la Warres through his sister, Joan, who had married John la Warre.

Our most substantial memorial to the la Warre family, a spiritual one, is the present cathedral. The last of that line, Thomas, applied in 1421 to reconstitute the parish church as a collegiate establishment under a warden. The first Warden of Manchester College was John Huntington and he began the process of rebuilding that was to be continued by his successors. The religious strife of the Reformation saw the dissolution of the priests' college in 1547, later acquired by the Earl of Derby, taken by the Commonwealth during the Civil War and eventually used by Chetham's trustees to house the Hospital and library. Elizabeth I granted a charter in 1578 and a series of Calvinistic appointments predisposed congregations to Puritan ideas. During the Cromwellian troubles Manchester took the Parliamentary side and in 1642 held out against a Royalist siege. The Diocese of Manchester was formed in 1847 and the church became a cathedral.

Manchester's third dynastic family, the Wests, sold the manor to mercantilism. A London clothworker, John Lacy, bought the rights in 1579 for £3,000, later reselling to Sir Nicholas Mosley. Mosley was a textile merchant trading from London with supplies from his brother in Manchester. After securing his fortune and a term as lord mayor, he returned to Lancashire in 1602. The Mosleys held the manorial rights until 1846 when the recently incorporated Manchester purchased the manor for £200,000.

The 17th century witnessed a transition from wool to cotton-based textiles. It has been said that 80 years before the Civil War, Manchester's reputation was made by wool and linen, and 80 years later the town was importing 2 million pounds of cotton from the East. Fortunes were made from the trade in fustians, calicos and muslins, none more celebrated than that of Humphrey Chetham whose benefaction still flourishes in the modern city.

Writing at the end of the 1700s, the local poet and historian James Ogden was able to assert that 'the large and populous town of Manchester, has now excited the attention and curiosity of strangers, on account of its extensive trade, and the rapid increase of its buildings with the enlargement of its streets; being also the theatre whereon the indefatigable Gilbert and ingenious Brindley exhibited their amazing talents'. The Bridgewater Canal, completed by Brindley in 1761, was indeed one of the wonders of the age. Even before that, the Mersey and Irwell had been made navigable as far as Hunt's Bank. The canal was later extended to Runcorn, giving the town access to waterway systems to the Midlands, as well as a route to the coast. At the start of the century, Manchester had a population of 10,000 and a feudal system of administration. At the dawn of the next 100 years, the town had acquired an exchange, infirmary, police commissioners, learned society, music concerts, Arkwright's spinning factory, John Dalton, and the Industrial Revolution. Its people numbered 70,000, yet still had a lord of the manor, Court Leet and no Parliamentary representation.

James Ogden was no believer in general enfranchisement, fearing the bribery and corruption which he believed such freedoms invited. His son, William, though, was a man of his times—a Lancashire Radical Reformer. The story of the Chartists and Peterloo is well known. The Reform Bill of 1832 did not bring universal suffrage, but it gave Manchester its first elected M.P.s: Mark Philips and Charles Thompson. Further political milestones were passed with the town's incorporation in 1838 following the Municipal Corporation Act three years earlier, and Manchester Corporation's acquisition of the manorial rights in 1846. The status of city was conferred in 1853 and of county borough in 1889.

Whereas late 19th-century Manchester was a city of merchants and warehouses, the early years had seen its manufacturing capacity grow apace. In 1802 there were 52 spinning mills, by 1830 this figure had almost doubled. In the 1820s a quarter of the UK spindles were to be found in the town. The population had reached 300,000 by the 1851 census, the squalor and overcrowding consequent on this causing much alarm.

Changing patterns of transport brought the railways in 1830 with the Manchester & Liverpool line. In 1824 the coach journey to London took 24 hours; nine years later the Telegraph's road time was 18 hours. Train times soon bettered these. By 1838 it was possible to reach the capital in 11 hours on the Grand Junction and London & Birmingham rail routes. London Road station opened in 1842. Traffic to Liverpool, Lancashire's industrial towns and Yorkshire was also vital to Manchester's key commercial role. The Manchester & Leeds Railway worked its trains into Hunt's Bank station (Victoria), opened in 1844. As the Edwardian age beckoned, rival train companies operated services into their own terminals: Victoria (Lancashire & Yorkshire); Exchange (London & North Western); Central (Cheshire Lines); London Road (Great Central and London & North Western).

Manchester's tramways started in 1877. These were operated privately until 1901, when the local corporation began its electric service. Horse power was abandoned two years later. Omnibus travel in and around Manchester goes back at least to the 1820s when John Greenwood's Pendleton equines hauled Mancunians through the town's streets. This parochial journeying was as nothing compared with the possibilities of Daniel Adamson's vision of a canal across the Cheshire plain to the sea. The Manchester Ship Canal was formally opened in 1894, linking the city to the ocean and the world. In two years the Trafford Park Estates Company had been formed, eventually to employ 50,000 people in 200 enterprises.

The 19th century sowed the seeds of today's sprawling 'donurbation', as the higher education complex has been colourfully dubbed. John Owens left money for the establishment of a seat of learning. Owens' College opened in 1851 at premises in Quay Street, once the home of Cobden. In 1880 it was one constituent of a federal university with Leeds and Liverpool; it had to await the new century before a charter created the Victoria University of Manchester. The Institute of Science and Technology began life more humbly as the Manchester Mechanics' Institute, founded in 1824. Elementary education was given a statutory framework in 1870 with the passing of Forster's Act. Manchester's first board-school was erected four years later in Vine Street, Hulme.

In 1881, a local industrialist was able to look back 50 years with the comment that the 'Saturday afternoon holiday, it was not even dreamt of'. Workers claimed the Saturday half-day as their own from mid-century onwards. In 1850, a Factory Act introduced a 60-hour week for women. Others in various industries then also sought and won this concession. Victorian Mancunians could use their recreation time in activity or indolence. The country's first public park maintained from the rates appeared in Manchester in the 1840s. An Art Treasures Exhibition was attended by over a million people in 1857. The Hallé music concerts were a direct consequence of the glittering event, but one victim of this showpiece was the Manchester Cricket Club, forced to vacate their ground near the present White City, for Lancashire's current headquarters.

Manchester is nothing if not a city of football. Little could the men of the Carriage and Wagon Department at the Newton Heath railway works have realised the titan they were launching when they formed their soccer team in 1878. Manchester City began playing as West Gorton Saint Mark's in 1880. The F.A. Cup final came to Manchester in 1893 when the crowds flocked to Fallowfield, home of the Manchester Athletic Club. Manchester played rugby football; League and Union. It ran, rambled, cycled, went to theatre, patronised the races, Whit-walked, imbibed the hops, and perhaps, after a gruelling week in office, shop or factory, just stayed at home and dozed.

Streets and buildings no more define a city than a body makes the person, but they do provide a matrix within which the organism breathes. The last century gave Manchester workshops, warehouses, factories and hovels. It also bestowed noble and dignified civic architecture. Alfred Waterhouse's Town Hall is a paradigm of Victorian Gothic. By the turn of the century, the street plan was 'modern'. The medieval village, huddled around the parish church, had evolved into a traffic-clogged industrial and commercial metropolis of 650,000 souls.

After Victoria . . . and Beyond

The dawn of the 20th century saw Manchester as *the* provincial city. It was the nucleus of the cotton industry; manufactured textile machinery; built locomotives and soon it would assemble motor-cars. Coal mines at Audenshaw (1881) and Pendleton (1904) fostered chemical production. Before the First World War Alliott Verdon-Roe produced aeroplanes near Great Ancoats Street. The trade slump of the 1870s and 1890s ended with Manchester braced for the recovery with its docks and Ship Canal. This improvement in world trade continued until the hostilities of 1914.

The Arts and Sciences prospered. Hans Richter came in 1899 to conduct the Hallé. The tradition of 19th-century experimental science exemplified by Dalton and Joule was maintained by the arrival of Ernest Rutherford as the university's professor of physics in 1907. His years of tenure saw Manchester scientists make pioneering discoveries in the embryonic discipline of sub-atomic physics. The Edwardian era also brought the country's first repertory company to Manchester, guided by Miss Horniman of the tea family.

Sporting Mancunians enjoyed early 20th-century success. Manchester City won the F.A. Cup in 1904, but were later involved in a scandal. Newton Heath adopted the name of Manchester United in 1902 and seven years later emulated their neighbours by also returning from the Crystal Palace with the 'tin god'. United played at Clayton until finding a more agreeable Old Trafford plot in 1910. City were at Hyde Road before transferring to the present ground. Like United, Lancashire Cricket Club found headquarters outside the city border. The tram or train journey to Old Trafford in 1904 was worth the fare. That season had the championship with the Red Rose as MacLaren led his side to 16 victories and no defeats. Rugby League's Challenge Cup went to Broughton in 1902.

Wish You Were Here

During the first two decades of this century, Britain was afflicted by a mania for picture postcards. It would be no great exaggeration to claim that there were pictorial cards of everything. They were collected, exchanged and preserved in decorated embossed albums. There they nestled: actresses and bishops; advertising; scenic idylls; seaside piers; cricketers and politicians; cemeteries and streets; birthday greetings; humour and disaster; religion and railways; markets and mayhem; not a sliver of life (and worse) escaped the attentions of the photographers, artists, publishers and salesmen. By the outbreak of war in 1914 over 900 million cards a year were posted in the UK. It was not only the numbers, but also the fine quality of much of the printing that has made posterity view this era as a 'golden age' of these rectangular mementoes.

Manchester, along with almost every other city, town, village and cross-roads fell victim to the postcard disease. This book offers a selection of images of Mancunian life during the early 20th century, in which many pictures derive from these cards. Most of the photographs date from before the First World War, although illustrations of the 1920s and 1930s are also interspersed. Postcard publishers ranged from giant companies with rotary presses and legions of employees, to one-man back-street photographers producing each card individually, the latter often with the more fascinating product. Whether from Valentine of Dundee or Ward of Oxford Road, they captured Manchester when it was still 'Cottonopolis', and the 'Mancunian Way' was simply London's way tomorrow.

The Plates

Greetings

1. Mancunian salutations; posted July 1906.

CONCILLO ET LABOR

MANCHESTER

Jaffa
REG? TRADE MARK.
HERALDIC SERIES.

2. Although Manchester was granted a charter as early as 1301, the town was governed by a feudal system until the 19th century. The Municipal Corporation Act of 1835 made provision for towns such as Manchester to become incorporated, with the power to levy rates, hold elections and sit in open council meetings. The charter of incorporation was won in 1838 and the manorial rights were purchased by the corporation from the Mosley family in 1846. The coat of arms was acquired in 1842. Manchester became a city in 1853 and in 1893 the first citizen took the title of Lord Mayor.

Politics and Civics

3. (*right*) Alfred Waterhouse's town hall building is considered one of Manchester's architectural treasures. The previous town hall was in King Street and later became the Free Reference Library. Its facade was re-erected in Heaton Park after the building was pulled down. The new civic home was opened by the mayor, Abel Heywood, on 13 September 1877. Ford Madox Brown produced a series of wall paintings for the Great Hall between 1876 and 1888. The extension was opened by King George in May 1938.

4. The Lord Mayor of Manchester introducing the entertainer Genevieve Ward to the guests at his garden party on 12 September 1917 in Heaton Park. The beneficiary of the fete was the East Lancashire Red Cross. Also in attendance was Harry Lauder and Master Francis Walsh, aged 10, the youngest piper in the world.

5. Daniel Defoe's observations that Manchester was 'the greatest mere village in England' and that 'they send no members to Parliament', were published in 1726. Over 100 years later, the 1832 Reform Bill provided for the return of Mark Philips and Charles Thompson as Manchester's first elected M.P.s, declared on 15 December of that year. The general election of 1906 that witnessed the defeat of a disunited Conservative Party by the Liberals, also saw a nascent Labour Party. John Clynes turned a Manchester North-east Tory majority of 706 in 1900 to a Labour victory by 2,432 votes. Born in Oldham, the son of an Irish labourer, he went on to hold office in the Labour governments of 1924 and 1929.

6. Arthur Balfour, the Tory Prime Minister between 1902 and 1905, represented Manchester East until his defeat in the 1906 general election. His name is associated with the Declaration on Palestine and he also steered the Education Act of 1902 through Parliament, creating local education authorities. He was a vice-president of Newton Heath F.C., later Manchester United.

7. The university's Fabian Society, continuing the tradition of Manchester's radical thinking, frozen by the camera in March 1917.

8. Manchester police officers, c.1905. An Act of 1792 established the town's commissioners, granting them various powers. Their duties not only involved the maintenance of a police force after dark, but also included cleansing, lighting and the laying of drains and sewers. In 1817 the commissioners built a local gasworks. There was, however, a general dissatisfaction with the old system of administration, although after incorporation the commissioners, church and court only reluctantly relinquished their rights in favour of the new authority. By the late 19th century a series of *ad hoc* bodies controlled health, highways, schools, burials etc. Modern local government structures only started to emerge with the 1888 Act, Manchester becoming a county borough the following year.

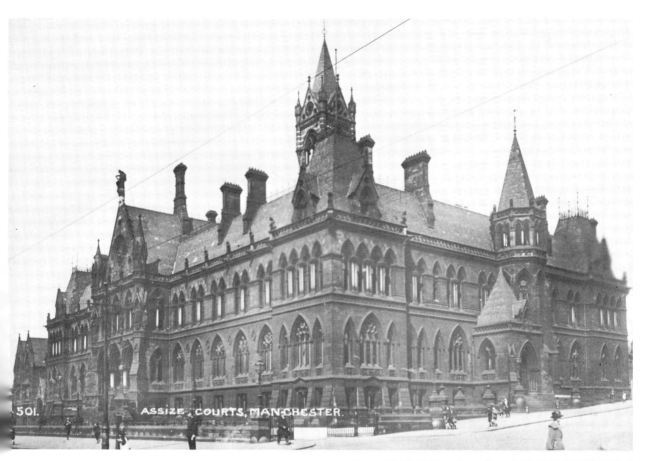

9. The Assize Courts, opened in 1859. This Victorian seat of judgement stood on Great Ducie Street in front of H.M. House of repentance at Strangeways. The building was bombed in 1940.

The gatehouse at Strangeways Prison in Edwardian days. The lock-up with its minaret tower has been a Manchester landmark since 1868.

New Fire Brigade Station, Manchester

11. The 'new' fire station on London Road and Fairfield Street was constructed in the years 1901-6. The pristine glory of its brick and terracotta later fell victim to Manchester's familiar dusky patina.

The Cathedral

12. Cathedral, Cromwell and the Belle Vue tram. Much of the present cathedral building dates from the 15th century. In 1421, the Rector of Manchester, Thomas de la Warre, obtained the right to reconstitute the former parish church as a collegiate church. The first warden, John Huntington, started the process of rebuilding. The la Warre baronial buildings were used as a priests' college and now house Chetham's music school. The tower was rebuilt in 1867. Cromwell's siting is apt. In Civil War times Manchester took the Parliamentary cause and in 1642 withstood a Royalist siege from across the nearby Irwell.

13. This 1930s view of the Cathedral gives some impression of the extraordinary width of the building. In 1940, bombing caused much damage; Manchester suffered more than any other English cathedral except Coventry. A 'Fire Window' commemorates the architect who undertook the restoration.

14.   The See of Manchester was created in 1847 with James Prince Lee confirmed as the first bishop. Edmund Knox, the fourth incumbent, succeeded to the bishopric in 1903 where he remained for 18 years.

Books and Learning

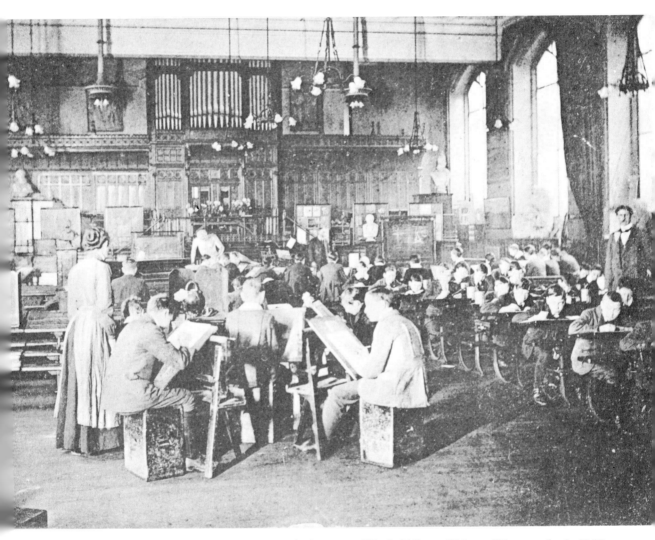

15. Manchester Grammar School's origin lies in the bequest of Hugh Oldham, Bishop of Exeter, who in 1515 gave family mills on the Irk to provide income to maintain a Free Grammar School. Attempts to establish a public school in the 1830s were thwarted by litigation, although fee-payers were admitted in 1867. These young Leonardos are sketching in the school's drawing hall when the buildings were in Long Millgate. The school left the city centre for more salubrious pastures in 1931.

16. The medieval buildings of Chetham's Hospital were presented by Thomas de la Warre, last in the line of Manchester's second feudal dynasty, to the collegiate church as a residence for clergy. That was in 1422. At the dissolution in Tudor times the buildings were taken by the Crown and offered to the Earl of Derby. In Cromwell's day they were seized by the Commonwealth, and later fell victim to neglect after use as a prison.

7. (*above*) Humphrey Chetham's monument stands in the Cathedral, uding one of Manchester's most noted benefactors. Chetham was ducated at the grammar school, proceeding to make his fortune as a anker and fustian merchant. He was appointed High Sheriff of ancashire in 1635, and once paid a fine for refusing a call from the ourt to be knighted. Although his scheme to open the old buildings s a 'hospital' or school for the children of 'honest, industrious and ainful parents' was never fulfilled in his own lifetime, the plan was nplemented by the trustees of his will. The hospital and a public brary were dedicated in 1656.

17a. (*right*) Dear Miss Gibson . . .

18. Boys of Chetham's Hospital in full livery, posing for the camera sometime during the 1930s. In 1969 girls were admitted for the first time. In the same year the foundation became a school of music.

19.   William Hulme's grammar school was established by the Hulme Trust in 1881. On Hulme's death in 1691, his original bequest was for four exhibitions at Brasenose College, Oxford. By the second half of the 19th century, the trust was so valuable that the Charity Commission granted its reorganisation and the foundation of schools in Manchester, Bury and Oldham.

20.   Manchester Girls' High School was endowed in 1874 by the Hulme Trust. This staff photograph was taken in November 1920.

21.   Manchester Girls' High School: this sylvan setting captures a moment during the 1921 production of the junior girls' *Midsummer Night's Dream*.

22. St Margaret's school, Manchester; Class 'G' with their teacher, Mr. Walker. The year inscribed on the reverse of the photograph is indistinct, although it appears to be 1911. There was lively debate on the role of voluntary or denominational organisations versus the local authority in the running of schools during the mid-19th century. The Lancashire Public Schools' Association (1847) felt that voluntary effort was too slow, and that large administrative areas were needed. The Manchester and Salford Committee on Education (1851) believed that such effort should be supported by the local administration. Forster's pioneering Act of 1870 ushered in the age of the school-board. Manchester's first board began life in December 1870. At first it was content to grant-aid voluntary schools from the rates, the first board-school being erected four years later in Vine Street, Hulme.

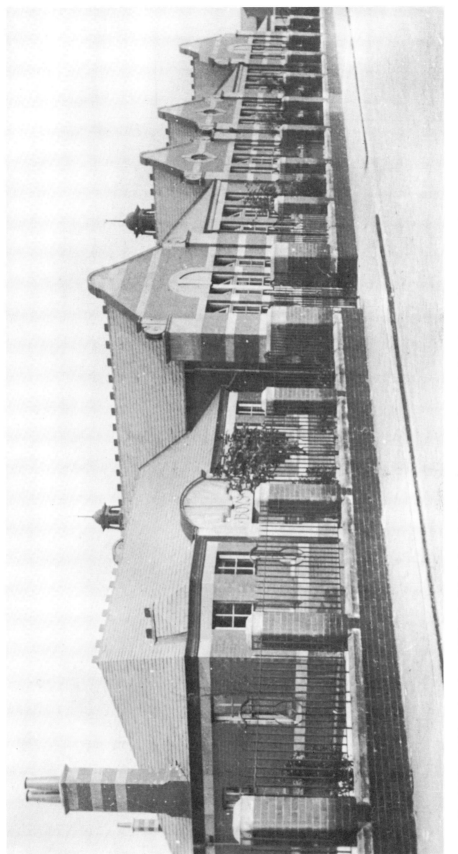

23. Balfour's Education Act of 1902 abolished the school-boards, transferring their functions to the county and county borough councils and so establishing local education authorities. This typical council school was photographed across the border in Stretford about 1908.

24.   Standard III, St Mark's, West Gorton, September 1905. As West Gorton St Mark's, the forefathers of
Manchester City F.C. played out their early battles in 1880, on the Kirkmanshulme cricket ground. They
later adopted the 'monikers' West Gorton, Gorton and Ardwick.

25.   As early as 1640 Manchester petitioned the Long Parliament for a northern university; Cromwell however decided in favour of Durham. In the next century higher learning was fostered through the Literary and Philosophical Society, founded in 1781, and a shortlived College of Arts & Sciences was established two years later. One early member of the 'Lit. & Phil.' was John Owens, a wealthy spinner, who on his death in 1846 bequeathed £96,000 for the establishment of a college. Owens' College began life in 1851, the trustees renting Cobden's old house in Quay Street, before moving to the present location in 1873. Waterhouse's Gothic edifice (seen here) was finished in 1902. A charter of 1880 created a federation with Liverpool and Leeds, and in 1903, reconstitution established the Victoria University of Manchester.

26. UMIST, as it is affectionately known today, evolved from the Mechanics' Institute which was founded in 1824. After 1882 it was designated the Manchester Technical School, and 10 years later came under the direction of the local corporation. This view of the main buildings was taken shortly after their opening in 1902. The modern institute is the university's Faculty of Technology.

27. Geological display, Victoria University, c.1905.

28. As befits a seat of learning such as Manchester, there is no dearth of libraries. Chetham's 17th-century foundation claims t[o] be the oldest public library in the country. [N]o less prized by Manchester and her scholars is the John Rylands memorial building and its collection, today an outpost of the universit[y] library. The Gothic structure was commissio[ned] by Mrs. Enriqueta Rylands in memory of he[r] late husband, a Wigan-born manufacturer. It was designed by Basil Champneys, and erec[ted] between 1890 and 1899. She paid £250,000 [to] Lord Spencer for the Althorp Library, and later bought 6,000 MSS. from the Earl of Crawford. It is said to house the finest collection of Bibles in the world.

The message on the back of this card reads; '*Dear Ted, I am sending you one of the views of Manchester where I work. You see the library – this is a new building just completed – in background you see the Town Hall. There is a big exten- n just started there as you will notice the hoarding up at the back of the Cenotaph.*' – October 1935.

. City Art Gallery, Mosley Street c.1935. The building was designed by Charles Barry, who also won the competition r the Houses of Parliament. Work was begun in 1824 for the Royal Manchester Institution, a learned body promoting ence and the arts. The City Art Gallery opened in 1883, today using the Athenaeum building, also by Barry, as an nexe. Its treasures include a splendid Pre-Raphaelite collection.

Medical Matters

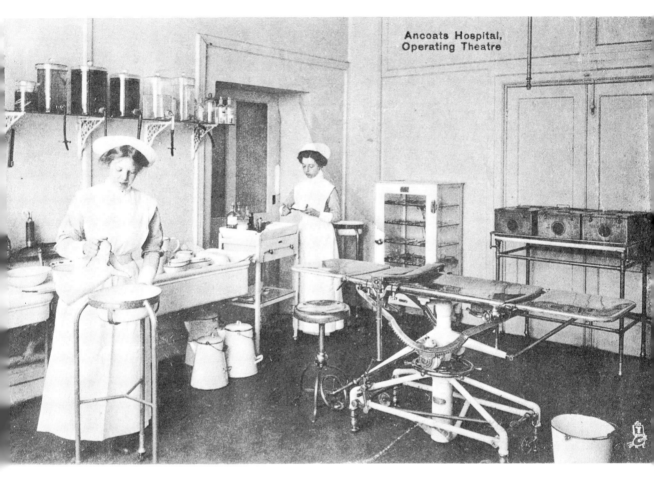

Ancoats Hospital,
Operating Theatre

31. (*opposite top*) Royal Infirmary, Piccadilly. Before the new hospital was built in Oxford Road, Piccadilly was dominated by the bulk of this pedimented pile. Manchester's first 'Publick Infirmary' was founded in 1752, and stood near the present Victoria station. It soon proved inadequate, and was relocated to this site, where it tended the sick for over 150 years. Nearly half of the founders of the Literary and Philosophical Society in 1781 were honorary physicians or surgeons at the infirmary, and Peter Mark Roget of 'Thesaurus' fame was appointed physician in 1804.

32. (*opposite below*) The new infirmary was ceremonially opened by the King and Queen on 6 July 1909. The style has been described by Pevsner as 'Greenwich Baroque'. Of the £500,000 cost, £400,000 came from the sale of the old Piccadilly site to Manchester Corporation, the balance through voluntary contribution.

33. (*above*) Ancoats Hospital, c.1900. Nurses preparing the operating theatre for a patient and surgeon.

Transport

(For further information about the construction of the Manchester Ship Canal, see plates 121 to 128.)

34. This prospect of the station approach is filled today by the sinuous frontage of Gateway House and the multi-storey offices of British Rail. London Road station opened in 1842, and was Manchester's first rail terminus for the lucrative London traffic. Although the London & North Western Railway held a monopoly on this market at first, rival companies soon appeared. The Great Central Railway shared the London Road facility with the L.N.W.R., each company working trains into their respective sides of the station. The Midland Railway also operated into London Road before routing its line to Manchester Central. Each enterprise sought to attract custom via fierce advertising, stressing scenic beauty, cost and, above all, speed. The station booking-hall seen in this photograph was demolished in 1959.

35. (*opposite above*) In 1913 Manchester's London Road station saw the end of the royal tour of Lancashire that had started a week earlier. King George and Queen Mary had been greeted in some 50 towns, before the state visit to Manchester on 14 July. The Lord Mayor of Manchester, Sir Walter Royse (having been dubbed in Albert Square earlier that day), here bids good-bye to the Euston-bound royal couple.

36. (*below*) The first Central Station was built in 1877 by the Manchester, Sheffield & Lincolnshire Railway (predecessor of the Great Central). Three years later the Cheshire Lines Committee (a grouping of the Midland, Great Northern and M.S.L.) built the single-arched structure familiar to all Mancunians. Central was the Midland's Manchester terminus from St Pancras, and also offered a route to Liverpool, rivalling the L.N.W.R. line from Exchange. The station never received a worthy frontage and closed in May 1969.

37.   Victoria Station first emerged as Hunt's Bank, opened in 1844. It provided Manchester's link to the industrial towns of Lancashire and Yorkshire, as well as communications with the port of Liverpool. Traffic outgrew its capacity, and the new Manchester Victoria was opened in 1884. Before the railway mergers of 1923, it was the home of the Lancashire & Yorkshire company, and a large tiled map of the L. & Y. still adorns one of its walls. This photograph, taken before the Great War, is easily recognisable as the Victoria of today.

38.   W.H. Smith & Son's railway bookstall, c.1910, Victoria Station.

39. A 1930s view of the area by the cathedral showing the driveway across the Irwell leading to Exchange Station. The east-west trains of the L.N.W.R. at first used the Hunt's Bank platforms, but the company opened its own Exchange terminus in the 1880s. The main buildings were bombed in 1940, although the station remained in operation until it was later 'rationalised'. One of its more spectacular features was the continuous platform with neighbouring Victoria, bridging the river and spanning 2194 ft. end to end.

40. Didsbury Station, c.1912. Manchester's railway network provided for the city's suburban hinterland as well as for inter-conurbation journeying. Victoria's platforms dispatched workers to their homes in Bury, Bolton, Oldham and all points in between. Didsbury was on the L.N.W.R.'s loop from the main line out of London Road. Opened in 1909, the track between Levenshulme and Wilmslow both relieved the main route and gave access to this region of south Manchester and Cheshire.

41. Richard Hoggart's 'gondolas of the people' first rumbled through the streets of Manchester in May 1877 when the corporation leased tracks to private operators. Although not originally permitted to run vehicles of its own, the council later sought powers to operate a fleet of local authority trams and the ceremonial opening of the Queen's Road depot took place on 6 June 1901. The system became all-electric in 1903 when the last horse routes were replaced. The last Manchester Corporation cars ran in January 1949. This photograph was taken in Oxford Street by the *Palace Theatre*.

At its peak, the Manchester tramway system was the most extensive outside London. Trams not only permitted travel the city suburbs, as this scene at Rusholme shows, but agreements with neighbouring operations allowed through journeys the towns of Ashton-under-Lyne, Oldham, Stockport, Rochdale and across the Irwell to Salford. By 1929 Manchester sted a fleet of 953 trams.

Piccadilly tram terminus in the 1930s.

44. A c.1930 view of Deansgate records the increasing impact of the private motor-car on modes of travel. It was la[ter?] observed of Deansgate that it appeared 'entirely given over to motor-car salesmen'. It seemed at one time as if the ca[r] industry would establish itself in Manchester. Mr. Rolls is reputed to have first met Mr. Royce in the *Midland Hotel*

he RR was built here before removal to Derby. (For further information about Rolls Royce Ltd., see plates 111 to
Ford cars were assembled at Trafford Park before 1929 when they moved to Essex.

PHOTO · BY
J. CLEWOR

ROYAL VISIT
TO MANCHESTER
JULY 14-19

45. For those eschewing more prosaic modes of transport, there was the regal splendour of an open carriage. Although Mancunian weather had threatened to dampen the occasion, the rain cleared as the royal couple plus the Earl of Derby headed a procession of 14 carriages from London Road Station, on the King and Queen's visit to Manchester in 1913. In Portland Street they were greeted by the voices of 15,000 children accompanied by the band from Chetham's Hospital, with their rendition of the national anthem.

46. (*opposite below*) The first Barton Aqueduct, a stone structure carrying the Bridgewater Canal over the Irwell, moved one 18th-century pensmith to verse.

> Vessels o'er vessels, water under water,
> Bridgewater triumphs—art has conquer'd nature.

When the Ship Canal was opened more than a century later, following the course of the river at Barton, this steel replacement was one of the engineering wonders of the Victorian age. Here we see a barge chugging along Brindley's canal above its 19th-century counterpart.

47. (*above*) Trafford swing bridge c.1915, closed to road traffic, delaying both man and horse. For further information about the Construction of the Manchester Ship Canal, see Plates 121 to 128.

8. Gunboat diplomacy might be id to have come to Manchester June 1929, when Commander S.V. Phillips headed his dest-yer flotilla along the canal to e docks. Perhaps not the traffic aniel Adamson and the Ship nal Committee had in mind, as ey fought opponents of the nal concept in the 1880s. Work rted in 1887, with a ceremonial ening in 1894. More than 30 ars later H.M.S. *Campbell* visited e port, bringing along her officer the watch, who, we are informed, cupied himself knitting socks.

Trade and Commerce

Section showing construction of walls an
Racecourse Grand Stand, shortly to be ot

49. With the Ship Canal came of course the Manchester docks, with their deep-water berths, cranes, warehouses and inter
railway system linked to main-line services. The construction of the large No. 9 dock was depicted on a series of postcards
this one shows the multi-gabled stand of the old racecourse in the process of demolition.

The impact of the docks on Manchester's growth has been illustrated thus—when work on the port began, Manchester
enough empty dwellings to house the whole of Stockport; after the canal had been in operation for 10 years, the houses
been filled and 10,000 new ones built. Maybe the city owed part of its success to bread—here we see two floating grain
ators at the No. 9 dock, and in the background is a fixed elevator with a capacity of 40,000 tons.

51. Trafford Park, overlooking the lake and part of the industrial complex. The Trafford Park Estates Company was formed in 1896. By 1932, a promotional booklet from the Manchester Development Committee was able to list over 170 enterprises located in this estate of 1,200 acres. Eventually 50,000 people found employment here, the Westinghouse Company building a small township for their employees.

52. Manchester has been called a 'city of middlemen'. The first Exchange was built by the lord of the manor, Sir Oswald Mosley, in 1729, and as well as being the centre of barter, it housed the Court Leet. This turn-of-the-century photograph shows Mills & Murgatroyd's 1874 building with its huge portico to Cross Street.

53. The present Royal Exchange was opened in 1921, ironically when cotton was in decline following a misread post-war boom. The floor of the building could accommodate over 10,000 members, and at 'High-Change' many of them were in evidence 'where merchants most do congregate'. Here we are offered a less fevered glimpse of the interior.

54. One 19th-century observer commented that 'once a city of mills, Manchester has now become a city of warehouses'. Pre-war Mancunians would have, no doubt, nodded agreement on viewing this backdrop to the Piccadilly Gardens. Destroyed in a bombing raid, these austere symbols of past prosperity gave way to today's concrete and glass Plaza.

55.   The Corn & Produce Exchange, c.1905.

CORN & PRODUCE EXCHANGE, MANCHESTER. 33.

56.   An animated and cobbled High Street from a postcard mailed in 1911. The Wholesale Fish Market to the left was opened in 1873. The old Smithfield Market is seen in the background.

MANCHESTER UNITED F.C.

Sporting Life

57. (*above*) Photographed at their recently opened Old Trafford ground, this portrays the 1911 Football League champions. Astride the ball sits their celebrated captain and Players' Union activist, Charlie Roberts. The secretary/manager J.E. Mangnall, who arrived in 1903, stands in fashionable boater to the right of the group.

58. The *Imperial Hotel* on Piccadilly was once known as the 'headquarters' of Manchester United. This souvenir postcard proclaims 'mine host' to be the club captain of their Newton Heath days, Harry Stafford. Stafford was in many ways the saviour of this famous side. Such was the parlous state of its finances in 1902 that a shareholders' meeting could only see a future if £2,000 was forthcoming. Up stepped Mr. Stafford with £500 of his own money and the names of four other backers. Newton Heath was reconstituted as the club of today, after this period of hovering on the brink.

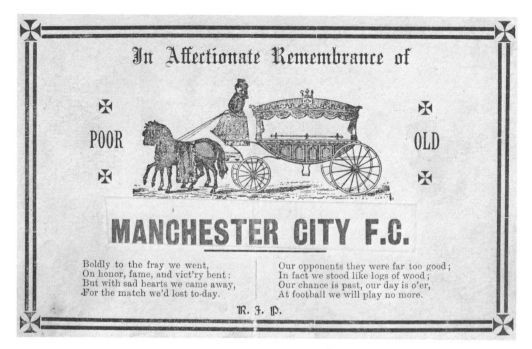

In Affectionate Remembrance of

POOR   **OLD**

MANCHESTER CITY F.C.

Boldly to the fray we went,	Our opponents they were far too good;
On honor, fame, and vict'ry bent:	In fact we stood like logs of wood;
But with sad hearts we came away,	Our chance is past, our day is o'er,
For the match we'd lost to-day.	At football we will play no more.

R. I. P.

59. Enough said!

60. Manchester City, 1903-4. Thanks to a goal by their captain Meredith, these 'Citizens' of 1904 returned to Manchester triumphant, after their 1-0 defeat of fellow Lancastrians Bolton Wanderers at the Crystal Palace. The winning goal was not without controversy, many Boltonians claiming that the hero was in an off-side position as he took the critical pass from his team-mate Livingstone. The glitter of success was later tarnished by F.A. investigations into allegations of illegal payments, transfer irregularities and bribery, leading to the suspensions of players and directors.

CUP FINAL AT MANCHESTER. "THE WINNING GOAL". "WHO GOT THAT GOAL"

61.   The palatial stadium at Old Trafford was open for business on 19 February 1910, when Liverpool were United's first guests, leaving with a 4-3 victory. The *Manchester Guardian* observed that 'the grandstand was a new luxury . . . with stewards to direct V.I.P.s to plush tip-up seats'. The following year, the F.A. decided that the setting was suitable for the re-played Cup-final between Newcastle and Bradford City, when the Yorkshiremen scored the only goal of the game. The cameraman behind the Stretford goal here captures the telling strike.

62.   Association football has a well-documented link with religious organisations. Indeed, several of today's professional clubs can trace their Victorian origins to the 'muscular Christianity' of the period. This group of eager athletes from the Fairfield Free Churches 2nd Team of 1911-12, photographed by J.W. Thorpe of Droylsden, are typical of the half-million amateur players who did battle in parks and fields all over the country during the early years of the century.

63. This 1920s aerial view of Fallowfield Stadium overlooks what can lay claim to be Manchester's most versatile sporting arena. Not only has it hosted athletics and cycle meetings, but both soccer and rugby football have been played here. In 1893 a crowd of 45,000 witnessed Wolverhampton Wanderers' single goal defeat of Everton in the first (non-replayed) F.A. Cup-final out of London. Six years later, Oldham and Hunslet clashed in the final of the Rugby League Challenge Cup.

BROUGHTON RANGERS. Manchester.

W. Harris	A. Hirst	Winskill	Gorry	Eddis	Davidson	Taylor (Tr.)
Barlow	Bouch	J. L. Clampitt	R. Clampitt	Lear
Mead	E. Jones	Warren

64. Rugby League football grew out of the dissatisfaction of several northern clubs with the English Rugby Football Union's attitude to 'broken-time payments'. In 1895, 20 teams seceded to form the Northern Rugby Football Union. Broughton were one of the original rebels, and went on to enjoy early success with the new organisation. Although this photograph is not dated, several of these players appeared in Broughton's 1911 Challenge Cup victory over Wigan. The club later moved to Longsight to play as Belle Vue, before withdrawing from the League in 1955.

HEAP. CUTTELL. KERMODE. TYLDESLEY. HALLOWS. SLADEN. SHARP. HAWKINS & BRIGHTON

LANCASHIRE CRICKET TEAM. (Professional.)

65. In the days when such things mattered, the Lancashire professionals of 1904 are seen here photographed apart from their 'gentlemanly' colleagues. This was championship season for the Red Rose, not least because of the flashing willow of England's leading pro. batsman Johnny Tyldesley, seen in the centre of the line-up. On the far right is Jack Sharp, who also played soccer for Everton and England.

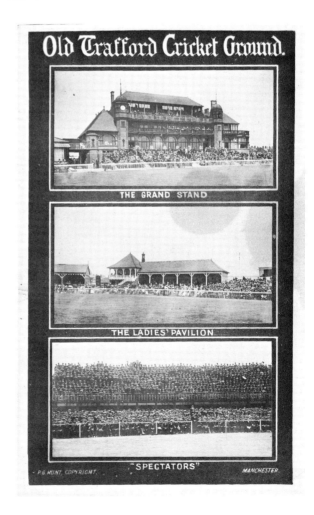

Old Trafford Cricket Ground.

THE GRAND STAND

THE LADIES' PAVILION

"SPECTATORS"

P.G. HUNT, COPYRIGHT.   MANCHESTER.

66. The present Old Trafford cricket ground was acquired by the Manchester Cricket Club and officially opened in June 1857. Their previous home, on the site of the White City, was lost to the Art Treasures Exhibition. The Lancashire club was the outcome of a meeting in 1864 at the *Queen's Hotel*, in which the Manchester C.C. and others submerged their separate identities. The first inter-county game at Old Trafford saw Middlesex vanquished by 62 runs.

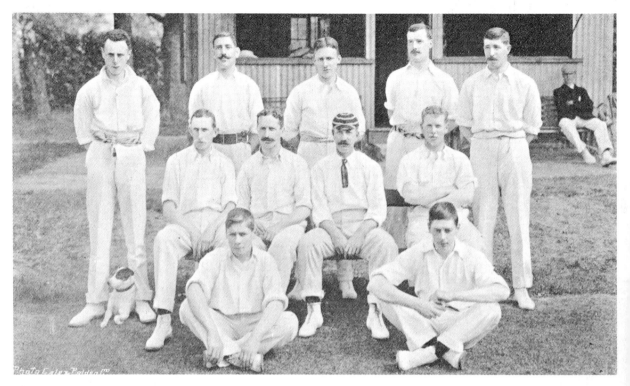

67. Cricketing soldiery (plus dog), from the 2nd Battalion Manchester Regiment, c.1905.

68. The Manchester Y.M.C.A. Harriers Joint Meet in January 1910 was preserved for posterity by this postcard. The eight teams of runners posed in comradely manner before the start at Alexandra Park, though the sender of the card complains of being tripped by a devilish rival after the 'off'.

Theatres and Cinemas

OXFORD STREET & PALACE THEATRE, MANCHESTER.

69.   The 'Palace Theatre of Varieties' is seen here in its Edwardian splendour. Built in the early 1890s by the Salford-born architect, Alfred Darbyshire, both the facade and auditorium have undergone several attempts at reconstruction and refurbishment. Threatened with closure in recent years, a Palace Theatre Trust has ensured its restoration and immediate survival.

70. A stroll or tram-ride to Oxford Street in the 1930s would have offered the latest celluloid attraction at the Paramount. During the week of this photograph, Hollywood's Magyar-in-residence, Paul Lukas, was starring in *The Beloved Bachelor*. Also, for those who preferred their entertainment live, Tom Burke and his 'Human Voice Orchestra' were filling the auditorium with their harmonies.

71. The message, date 1907, on the reverse o this postcard of the ol Hippodrome revealed i to be 'the largest music Hall in M'r. Two per-formances nightly'. Opened in 1904, it wa designed by that proli-fic theatre architect, Frank Matcham, but in the 1930s the old boards surrendered to the changing taste.

72. A typical example of suburban theatre and cinema of bygone days was the Alhambra at Higher Openshaw.
A perambulation along Ashton Old Road brought welcome relief from the drudgery of the working day with
pictures twice nightly. Matinees were also on offer three days a week. Opened in 1908, the auditorium has been
described as 'dull and fan-shaped'.

Musical Manchester

73. (*above*) The name of the Free Trade Hall, one of Manchester's most famous buildings, is resonant with the political history of 19th-century England. The first hall, built of wood, was erected at St Peter's Field, on land given by Cobden. The present structure dates from the 1850s, although large scale restoration work was needed after the last war. The committee of the 1857 Arts Exhibition invited Charles Hallé to enlarge the Gentlemen's Concerts Orchestra, which had existed since the 1770s. When the exhibition closed, Hallé resolved to keep the orchestra together, and inaugurated his concerts in the Free Trade Hall in January 1858.

74. Charles Hallé first arrived in Manchester in 1848, at the invitation of one of the directors of the Gentlemen's Concerts. Appointed conductor in 1850, he improved the orchestra and, for the 1857 Exhibition, gave a series of daily concerts. Under his baton, music in Manchester flourished, and his death in 1895 was the occasion for a display of civic mourning.

75. Besses O'th Barn Band, c.1905.

75a. Detail of Plate 75 above.

Belle Vue

76.   Belle Vue has entertained Mancunians since 1836 when the pleasure garden was opened, 'promoted by the energy and enthusiasm' of John Jennison. This entrance admitted Edwardian fun-seekers to a world of exotic beasts and big dippers. Manchester hedonists have also journeyed to Longsight in search of wrestling and oratorio, circus and speedway.

77. Belle Vue's most notorious ride was the famous Bobs Coaster, with its record-breaking velocity down the first incline. Built in 1929 by an American, H. E. Traver, the 'fear-machine' was sold for scrap in 1970. This photograph shows an early century antecedent—the Belle Vue Figure-8 Toboggan.

78. Monkey business at tea-time! Belle Vue c.1905.

White City

79.   In 1907, 6d. (2½p.) gained admission to the White City pleasure park. This imposing entrance, with its Ionic columns and classical sculpture, was the gateway to grounds that had been the site of the grand Art Treasures Exhibition half-a-century before. A botanical garden flourished in earlier times, and the Manchester Cricket Club's first Old Trafford wicket was rolled here before their forced migration to the present Lancashire headquarters.

. White City; 'The Great Water Chute', 1907.

81.   White City, 1907; helter-skelter and side-shows.

82. Engels' classic account of Manchester slum life in the 1840s paints a picture of unrelieved squalor in an asphyxiated city. The banker, Benjamin Heywood, the first president of the Manchester Statistical Society, and Mark Philips, one of Manchester's first M.P.s, acted to provide 'lungs for the congested districts'. In 1846 they created Queen's Park and Philips Park, the first public parks in Britain supported from the local rate. These 60 acres were the start of a policy that has given Manchester over 90 parks and gardens. This photograph of the fountain in Philips Park dates from c.1910.

83. Manchester acquired the 638 acres of Heaton Park in 1902. The Georgian hall was designed for the Earl of Wilton in 1772. The disembodied facade of the old King Street town hall was re-erected by the lake after the building's demolition in 1911.

84. This arboreal scene is the entrance to the 1908 Royal Lancashire Agricultural Show, held in Platt Fields over the August Bank Holiday weekend. Events included 'machinery in motion', flower and vegetable displays, livestock racing and horses 'leaping over hurdles'.

85. Manchester ramblers stretching their legs by Gorton reservoir, during the early years of the century.

86. An Edwardian fashion show in the sun by the lakeside in Platt Fields.

87. Officers of the Manchester Battalion of the Boys' Life Brigade at Abergele Camp, 1913. This organisation disappeared in 1926 after merger with the rival Boys' Brigade, when the latter had abandoned its use of rifles in the Christian fight.

Bibles and Bugles

88. Whit Walks were ever a popular Manchester tradition—or at least since the first processionists departed St Ann's Square in 1801. This parade of young marchers negotiating the cobbled highway was snapped by the Newton Heath photographer, Pearson, whose studio was in Oldham Road.

Mancunian Ways

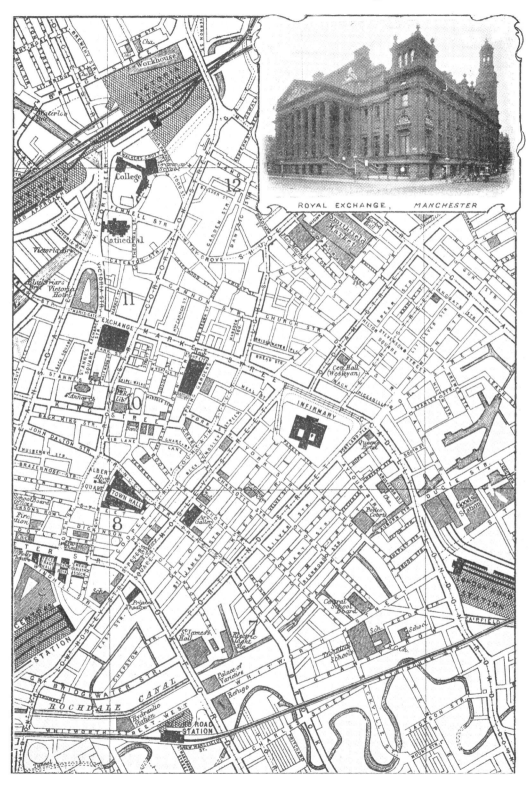

ROYAL EXCHANGE, MANCHESTER

89. A city centre street map c.1900. The *Midland Hotel* is not yet built; the Free Reference Library stands in King Street; and the Royal Infirmary is located in Piccadilly.

90. The *Seven Stars* in Withy Grove boasted of being the oldest licensed inn in Britain, county records giving the date as 1356. The Court Leet accounts speak of a priest in 1571 imbibing during service time by popping down to the local, via a secret passage linking the hostelry with the collegiate church. 'Last orders' were shouted in 1911 when the building was pulled down.

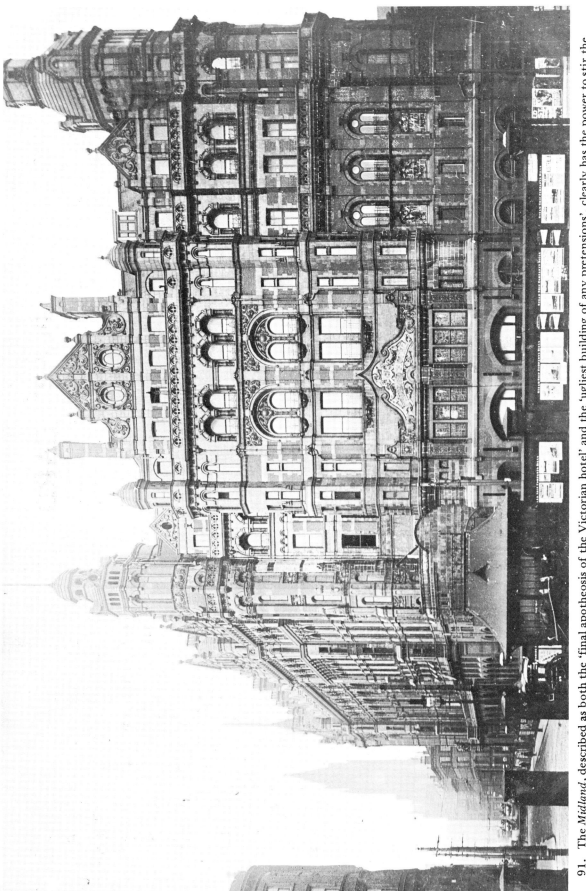

91. The *Midland*, described as both the 'final apotheosis of the Victorian hotel' and the 'ugliest building of any pretensions', clearly has the power to stir the sensibilities. Designed by Charles Trubshaw and built between 1898 and 1903, its Gentlemen's Concert Hall staged Miss Horniman's early dramatic productions in Edwardian Manchester. Rolls and Royce first met here and Mario Lanza, Sarah Bernhardt and countless visitors to Cottonopolis down the decades have enjoyed its grandeur.

92. Market Place, looking towards the cathedral. This part of old Manchester has mostly succumbed to the developers' concrete and glass. The timber-framed building is the *Wellington Inn*, which was later lifted in order to be placed in its present incongruous site.

93.   The *Wellington Inn*, c.1900. The poet John Byrom was born here in 1692, the son of a linen-draper. After Cambridge, he returned to Manchester, writing among other things, 'Christians Awake', and applying his medical skills when not brandishing the quill.

94. St Ann's was, seemingly from this scene, one of the city's most 'hansom' squares. In earlier times the area was know
as Acresfield and the location of a medieval fair.

95. A turn-of-the-century vignette of King Street, highlighting Goodwin's old town hall
building, erected between 1819 and 1834. It later served as a reference library and, on
demolition, the facade was preserved in Heaton Park.

96. Edwardian days in Market Street, viewed from St Mary's Gate. The tower of the Royal Exchange soars high above man, tram and beast.

97. Poet's Corner, Long Millgate: Davis's antique shop.

98. This busy street scene is almost unrecognisable to the modern eye. We are standing at the end of Exchange Str
looking in the direction of the cathedral. Across the way is a section of Victoria Street that has now become a mem
The building on the left is one corner of the *Victoria Hotel*, that once occupied a triangular area bounded by Victor
Street, Deansgate and St Mary's Gate.

99. The growth of motorised transport during the inter-war years is all too apparent from the congested scene in Market Street. This contrasts as dramatically with today's petrol-free walkway, as does the modern shopping monolith of St Arndale with yesteryear's variegated architecture.

MARKET STREET, MANCHESTER.

"Philco" Series.

100. Market Street is one of Manchester's oldest thoroughfares and appears on a plan of the town, published in 1822 but showing the topography of 170 years earlier. It was then known as Market Stead Lane. This shot of the street's horse-power was taken from near the Royal Exchange at the turn of the century.

101. Cross Street, c.1910. The portico on the left belongs to the Royal Exchange, later to give way to its successor. Opposite we see the offices of the *Evening News* and *Manchester Guardian*; the latter under the editorship of its most famous helmsman, C. P. Scott, who arrived in 1872 at the invitation of the owner, who was also his cousin.

CROSS STREET, MANCHESTER.

102   Cross Street, late 1930s

PICCADILLY, MANCHESTER.

103. The first infirmary moved to Piccadilly in the 1750s to escape the clamour of the growing town near the church. Prints show the new building amid fields and flowers. When the Royal Infirmary moved on again, this time to Oxford Road, Piccadilly had become the hub of a great industrial and commercial city. The area was once called Lever's Row.

104. An Edwardian and bustling Oldham Street. The tram is making for Oldham Road and on to Hollinwood.

105. 'Nothing over 6d.'! Frank Winfield Woolworth's revolutionary idea on retailing came to Piccadilly in 1929, with the opening of the '3d. and 6d. store' on the corner of Oldham Street. Woolworth was an American, and the first store under his own name traded in Lancaster, Pennsylvania. Lancashire, England was chosen for the British experiment; the first shop, in Liverpool, appeared in 1909.

106. Oxford Street, c.1930. To the left the Hippodrome invites, and beyond is the Prince's Theatre. In the far distance, St Peter's Square has its Cenotaph but as yet no library.

107.   A rather unfamiliar St Peter's Square in the distance as we cast a glance from Oxford Street. The camera is pointing in the direction of today's Central Library. The nearest tower belongs to the now demolished St Peter's church; behind rises that of the town hall.

108.   St Peter's Square, before the Central Library and Town Hall extension projects of the 1930s altered the scale of architecture. The Cenotaph dates from 1924 and was designed by Sir Edwin Lutyens.

109. Old-time soccer managers could have found less doughty line-ups than the five strung out across Albert Square. Although Gladstone may have demurred at his right-wing spot, Bright at left of centre should feel more comfortable.

110. Deep depression!

Pleasant Weather AT MANCHESTER

111. The crane section shop at the new Royce Ltd. factory, Trafford Park, c.1900.

The Early Days of Rolls Royce Ltd.

112. The foundry shop at the new Royce Ltd. factory, Trafford Park, c.1900.

113.   The first Rolls Royce petrol engine on test, September 1903.

114.   The first Royce prototype 2 cylinder 10 H.P. car first took to the road on 1 April.

115. A 2 cylinder, 10 H.P. Rolls-Royce car of 1905.

116. The tool room group in the Cooke Street works of Rolls Royce, c.1904.

117.   The original works of Rolls Royce, Cooke Street, Hulme, 1937.

118.   The Blake Street entrance to the Cooke Street works of Rolls Royce, 1939.

119. An interior of the Triangle Works, Cooke Street.

120. The Cooke Street area after the Second World War.

The Manchester Ship Canal

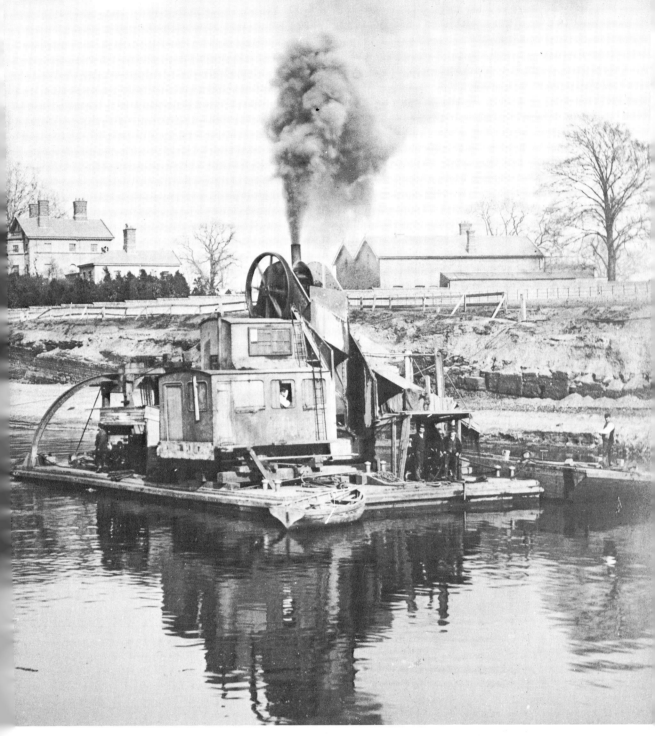

121. (*opposite above*) Latchford High Level railway bridge, c.1890.
122. (*opposite below*) Engines on a bridge over the canal, c.1890.
123. (*above*) This unusual vessel was photographed in 1890.

125, 126. The picture above, taken in the 1890s, shows the scale of construction work on the canal at that time, while the scene below is typical of turn-of-the-century canalside squalor. Note that in both pictures all work stops to pose for the camera.

127. The Manchester Ship Canal at Warrington in the 1890s.

128. The formal opening of the Manchester Ship Canal by Queen Victoria in the *Enchantress*, 21 May 1894.